# Timeless Colours Waterford

PEMBROKE

IAN HANNIGAN

# Timeless Colours
# Waterford

First published in 2024 by
Merrion Press
10 George's Street,
Newbridge,
Co. Kildare,
Ireland
www.merrionpress.ie

This edition first published in 2024



9781785375279 (Hardback)
9781785375316 (Ebook)

A CIP catalogue record for this book is available from the British Library.



Typeset in Georgia Pro, Brandon Grotesque and Mala.

Cover and internal design by Padraig McCormack

Front cover image: **THE CLOCK TOWER**, Waterford, known as 'Port Lairge' in Irish, is captured beautifully in this centre feature. The single panel from a stereoscopic image depicts the simplicity of working life on Waterford Quay showcasing impressive tall ships, and bustling activity, all on what appears to be a fine day.

Back cover image: **DROMANA GATE AND BRIDGE**, *c.*1870. The Dromana Hindu-Gothic Gate and Bridge are located near Villierstown. Today, it stands as a unique architectural gem in Ireland.

**Opening credits**

***THE SS PEMBROKE***, 18 February 1899, The vessel was operated by the Great Western Railway route, and regularly sailed from Milford Haven to Waterford. The vessel ran aground on 18 February 1899 off the Wexford coast. Once repaired, it operated for another 25 years before retirement.

**BAKING THE BLAA**, *c.*1896, Adair's Bakehouse, Waterford city. The rich, warm hues belie the age of the image, evoking the tantalising aroma of freshly baked bread and batches of the famous Waterford 'blaa' (seen top middle). It's a scene that undoubtedly captures the ambiance of early morning and an age-old Waterford tradition that has stood the test of time.

**WOMAN AND DONKEY**, 1928, Kilmeaden, Co. Waterford. A charming snapshot of Gretta Sullivan, a neighbour to and supplier of Kilmeaden Creamery, riding the milk cart with a bright smile. Taken on 31 May 1928, this image evokes a sense of joy and simplicity in everyday rural life.

**JIM WARE**, 1948, Ware was captain of the Waterford senior hurling team and a key figure in their 1948 All-Ireland Hurling Championship victory. Ware would go on to serve as a selector for the winning side of 1959. At the age of forty, he became the oldest All-Ireland winning captain.

Merrion Press is a member of Publishing Ireland

## Acknowledgements

I would like to thank *Old Ireland in Colour* co-author John Breslin from the University of Galway for his continued advice, friendship and support, leading up to and since my decision to create this book. Mary Frances Ryan, Editor of *Waterford News & Star* has been a steadfast supporter of *Timeless Colours*, publishing my work numerous times in the *Waterford News & Star* newspaper and in the Christmas Annual. Willie Whelan from Waterford County Museum for his advice, assistance, collaboration and continued support. Janet Carey of the Lafcadio Hearn Japanese Gardens in Tramore, Waterford and to Ann Cusack of the Granville Hotel Waterford for their ongoing support and shared passion for Lafcadio Hearn and Thomas Francis Meagher respectively. Waterford Councillor Mary Roche (SDP) and former Mayor of Waterford city, for her advice and support. Joanne Rothwell, Waterford city and County Council Archivist, for her advice and support. Additional thanks to the National Library of Ireland, Irish Museum of Childhood, steadfast supporters of my work John Bray, Liam Cahill (RIP), Val Flynn, David Rogers, Damien Geoghegan and Eugene Falconer and to all of you, for your enduring support and encouragement for all things *Timeless Colours* and Waterford. I especially want to thank my family and friends in Ireland and Germany for their unending encouragement and support. I dedicate this work to them and to the proud people of Waterford, past, present, and future.

## About the Author

**Ian Hannigan** is a Waterford native who now lives in Berlin, Germany with his partner, Susanne, and their dog, Lela. He works as a designer and entrepreneur, having started two technology companies, one in Ireland and one in Germany. For over two decades he's held key creative positions at leading companies in Ireland, Germany and the UK. His work has been enjoyed by millions of people around the world. He's been a long-term mentor to high-potential startups through the Techstars Ecosystem in Germany and Italy. Ian started Timeless Colours online in 2020 out of a combined passion for cutting-edge technology, design and a fascination with historical photographs, especially those focused on the rich history of Waterford.

Follow Ian's latest work shared on X, Facebook and Instagram under @timelesscolours.

VISITORS
ARE
INVITED
TO
INSPECT

## Waterford City and County

Waterford is located in Ireland's sunny south-east. It is commonly known as 'The Déise' after its ancient Gaelic settlers. The region's history is etched into its landscape, from ancient ring forts and early Christian monastic sites to the rugged Copper Coast, shaped by centuries of mining. These lands whisper tales of Viking invasions, Norman conquests, and resilient communities that have weathered countless adversities. Waterford's rich history plays an indelible role in Ireland's past, present and future.

Founded by Vikings in 914 CE, central Waterford holds the title of Ireland's oldest city. It quickly became a pivotal trade and commerce hub, with the River Suir facilitating the movement of goods. Over the centuries, the city evolved into an industrial powerhouse, renowned for its brewing, glass-making, and textiles. Its coastal position also made it a strategic point of contention, witnessing numerous battles and sieges.

Dungarvan and Lismore towns, with their historic castles, serve as beacons of the county's enduring importance in Ireland's overarching history. As the twentieth century dawned, Waterford city emerged as a political epicentre during the Irish War of Independence and later the Civil War, producing key figures in the fight against British dominion.

Ultimately this is a tale of two cities, highlighting divisions between prosperity and marginalisation, empowerment and disempowerment, and the time before and after the 1916 Rising. *Timeless Colours: Waterford* focuses on the period 1840–1960, capturing more than a century of transformative change.

Reginalds Tower, c.1890s, The Mall, Waterford

## Colourisation and Restoration

In a world where history often feels like a distant, academic subject, *Timeless Colours: Waterford* offers an invitation to see and experience the past as if you were there witnessing the event. This book is a testament to the power of combining advanced colourisation and restoration technology with meticulous research and artistry. Each black and white image is painstakingly restored, with colours added, tweaked, or emphasised by hand. The result is a harmonious spectrum of colour and light which not only captures, but enhances, the vibrant hues that existed in the original scenes.

Why undertake this process at all? Some critics even argue that colourisation is purely 'fake', yet clearly the emotions these images evoke in the viewer are profoundly real. Besides being an enjoyable creative outlet, the impact of colourisation extends far beyond mere visual appeal. The process of colourisation sparks curiosity and fosters a deeper appreciation for the stories that have shaped our history. In doing so, it breaks down the barriers often erected by history's gatekeepers, who sometimes present the past in ways that can feel removed or inaccessible or even distorted. Films like Peter Jackson's *They Shall Not Grow Old* have highlighted how technology through the use of engaging images can bring history and its people back to life for a whole new audience. There are many ways of using media to explore history, this is just one of them. No one group owns history, it belongs to everyone.

As the technology matures, so does our ability to connect with history in a more immediate and tangible way. Each image in this book resonates with a special connection to the place and people it captures.

Whether you're a devoted historian, a casual history buff, a proud Waterfordian or someone who simply appreciates artistic craftsmanship, this book aims to dissolve the barriers between then and now. Not only an artistic endeavour; it's an invitation to experience history as a living, breathing world.

For those readers with an eagle-eye, you may even notice a white and blue colour combination recurring throughout many images — an easter egg of sorts, honouring Waterford's emblematic white and blue colours.

Apple Market Boys, c.1900, Waterford

# 1840–1880

## Young Irelanders Under Arrest

1848, Kilmainham Gaol, Dublin

Leone Glukman's incredibly rare daguerreotype image of 'Young Irelanders' William Smith O'Brien and Thomas Francis Meagher, flanked by their gaoler and a soldier, while on death row at Kilmainham Gaol.

They were jailed for the Young Ireland Rebellion in 1848, which involved the first ever defiant flight of the Irish Tricolour from 33 The Mall, Waterford.

It was a crime that resulted in Meagher and O'Brien initially sentenced to death (by being hung, drawn and quartered), which was later converted to penal servitude for life and hard labour on Van Diemen's Land (now Tasmania), from which Meagher would famously escape to fulfill his destiny.

## An Gorta Mór

c.1856, Lismore, Co. Waterford

The oldest known photo of a survivor of The Great Hunger (1845–1852), this man was an unknown labourer who lived through and survived An Gorta Mór, or the Great Famine as it's otherwise known. On an ambrotype photograph, he is seen smoking his pipe, he's believed to have worked as a labourer on the Devonshire Estate in Lismore, Co. Waterford. The catastrophe was the greatest loss of life in western Europe in the 100 years between the Napoleonic Wars and World War I. We can only imagine the horrors he must have witnessed.

## Thomas Francis Meagher

c.1860–1865, New York, USA

A rare photograph of the legend that is Thomas Francis Meagher with cap raised aloft in triumphant salute - as if to mark the first flight of the Irish Tricolour in Waterford just twelve years earlier in 1848.

Thomas Francis Meagher (1823–1867), Irish nationalist, soldier, and leader of the Young Irelanders in the Rebellion of 1848. Born in Waterford, Meagher became a vocal advocate for Irish independence from British rule. His involvement in the 1848 rebellion led to his conviction for sedition, after which he was sentenced to death, commuted to life in exile in Van Diemen's Land (now Tasmania).

In 1852 Meagher escaped to the United States, where he became a prominent figure in the Irish-American community. With the outbreak of the American Civil War in 1861, he formed the Irish Brigade and fought for the Union, rising to the rank of Brigadier General. Meagher was appointed Acting Governor of the state of Montana. However, his tenure was cut short when he mysteriously disappeared in 1867.

Beyond his military and political achievements, Meagher is best remembered in Ireland for introducing the Irish Tricolour, which later became the national flag. His legacy as a champion of Irish and Irish-American causes endures to this day.

## The Clock Tower

c.1870, The Quay, Waterford

Waterford, known as 'Port Láirge' in Irish, is captured beautifully in this centre feature. The single panel from a stereoscopic image depicts the simplicity of working life on Waterford Quay showcasing impressive tall ships, and bustling activity, all on what appears to be a fine day.

## Dromana Gate

c.1870, Dromana, Co. Waterford

The Dromana Hindu-Gothic Gate and Bridge are located near Villierstown. The gate was originally built from wood and papier mâché and constructed as a welcome home gift by the village tenants to the owner of the Dromana Estate near Cappoquin, Henry Villiers-Stuart and his new wife, Theresia Pauline Ott of Vienna. The couple had returned from their honeymoon in Brighton in 1826, where they were enamoured by the Royal Pavilion designed by John Nash. The gate was inspired by Nash's Indo-Saracenic-style pavilion, and was reconstructed in stone around 1830. Today, it stands as a unique architectural gem and the best surviving example of this style of architecture in Ireland.

## The Square

c.1870–1887, Portlaw, Co. Waterford

Robert French captures 'The Square' in Portlaw, Co. Waterford. Established by the Malcomson family in 1825. This Quaker Model Village, the only one in Ireland, adhered to three guiding principles, often referred to as the '3 Ps': no pubs, no pawn and no police.

# 1880–1900

## The Draper's Wife

c.1880s, Tramore, Co. Waterford

Mr Joe Tobin and Mrs Nannie Tobin. Joe Tobin was a draper by profession. This moment was captured at Rocklands in Tramore.

A tragic note accompanies this image, as recorded in the *Kilkenny Moderator* on 26 May 1917:

> Joseph Tobin passed away in 1902. Following his death, his wife Nannie and three of their children relocated to London. Tragically, in 1917, all four of them perished in a house fire. The funeral was attended by their surviving children.

## Asylum

c.1880, John's Hill, Waterford

The refectory of the Waterford District Lunatic Asylum, located on John's Hill, now known as St Otteran's Hospital, holds stories of its past. In this scene, Dr Ringrose Atkins and the Superintendent are visible at the back, while a patient can be seen sitting next to the stove on the left. If only those walls could speak ...

DGAA

## Dan Fraher

c.1880, Dungarvan, Co. Waterford

Dan Fraher was an athlete, GAA administrator, Irish language activist, and the inventor of early GAA sports costumes, as showcased in this image. He was the original proprietor of the Gaelic grounds in Dungarvan, which has since been renamed 'Fraher Field' in tribute to his legacy.

## Lafcadio Hearn

24 August 1888, Martinique Island, Lesser Antilles

Patrick Lafcadio Hearn (1850–1904) was born in Greece and moved to Rathmines, Dublin, as a young child. He spent his summer holidays with relatives in Tramore, Co. Waterford. While he remains virtually unknown in Ireland, Lafcadio is a revered figure in Japan and other parts of the world, particularly for his children's book of ghost stories, *Kwaidan: Stories and Studies of Strange Things* (first published in 1904). He wrote fourteen books in total, becoming the leading interpreter of Japan's rich culture for Western readers. The beautiful Lafcadio Hearn Japanese Gardens in Tramore celebrate his legacy and connection to Waterford.

## Broad Street

c.1890, Broad Street, Waterford

In this snapshot by Robert French, a lively town is shown on Broad Street, also known as John Roberts Square. The scene is alive with shops and eager townspeople. Children can be seen playing, while a gentleman, hands clasped behind his back, walks away deep in thought. We can only offer a penny for those thoughts, long-since thought.

FURNITURE BEDSTEADS BEDDING & IRONMONGERY
D. SLANEY

L. & N. TEA Co
THOMAS ROBERTS
VICTUALLER

## The Mall

c.1890, The Mall, Waterford

A truly iconic view of Waterford showing people going about their everyday lives on The Mall, over 130 years ago, lives which are captured forever through this work by Robert French.

SD
JOHN DUNCAN
SON & CO
JOHN DUNCAN
SON & CO
LIVERPOOL
JOHN DUNCAN
SON & CO

## Dunmore Pier

c.1890, Dunmore, Co. Waterford

This image, taken by Poole, depicts a busy day in the picturesque fishing village of Dunmore East. The photograph shows a thriving industry with goods in crates and barrels recently arrived from Liverpool getting ready to be transported by horse and cart to various towns in Waterford.

## Ballybricken Fair Day

c.1890, Ballybricken, Waterford

A remarkable shot by A.H. (Arthur Henri) Poole shows a bustling Fair Day on Ballybricken, as created for and featured on a postcard of the time.

## Alive, Alive Oh!

c.1892, Tramore, Co. Waterford

On Strand Road (looking towards the station end) in Tramore, Co. Waterford, a rare portrait of a Cockle Seller. She appears to be pregnant, holding her hand to protect her unborn child from the camera, a superstition of the era. She represents the many Waterford women who sold cockles for generations.

The familiar lyrics of 'Molly Malone' ring out:

Alive, alive oh
Alive, alive oh
Crying, "cockles and mussels,
alive, alive oh"

## The Men's Slip

c.1890s, Tramore, Co. Waterford

At the bathing slip in Tramore, Co. Waterford, there's a striking display of early twentieth-century male swimwear. Some of the designs appear so unique that they almost seem like impromptu creations.

3
9

## Cockle Pickers

c.1890, Woodstown Strand, Co. Waterford

Woodstown Strand, Poole snaps a group of cockle pickers, women and girls, alongside a donkey and cart. From left to right, the children are Ellen Henry, Jane Henry and Katie Henry standing in front of the cart. They stopped daily and prayed the Angelus at noon, when the bells rang in nearby Duncannon.

## The Poole Family

c.1890, Poole Studio, Waterford

A fascinating group portrait of the extended Poole family. Arthur Henri, abbreviated to A.H., and Elizabeth are centre, nephew Bernard Poole right, children Violet, Bertram and Vyvyan front. Mr Samuel Poole and his wife to the left, behind the very Victorian 'fainting sofa'.

Elizabeth's connection with Dr Mary Strangman, through her father's profession as a builder to the Strangmans, may have contributed to the initial and continued success of the Poole Photographic Firm in Waterford. The Strangman family were one of the leading business families in Waterford in the nineteenth and twentieth centuries. The studio was active from around 1884 to around 1954. Poole's photographic works captured the life and events in the Waterford area during that period. The famous collection includes photographs of local people, social events, sports, businesses and various scenes.

## Bathing Box Lady

c.1890s Tramore, Co. Waterford

In Tramore, a determined lady works alongside her husband, managing the bathing boxes, a place where shy bathers could change into their swimming costumes. She has a dudeen, or woman's pipe, in her mouth. Large stones are strategically placed just behind the wheels of the bathing boxes to prevent them from rolling away.

## The Bells

c.1890s, Poole Studio, Waterford

A.H. Poole's striking photograph showcases Mr Henry Bell's family from The Quay, Waterford, dressed more modestly than one might expect for such portraits.

Their attire reflects traditional Quaker practices, where simplicity in clothing wasn't just a style choice. Quakers often opted for plain garments as a form of defense, hoping to avoid drawing unwanted attention. Such beliefs even extended to details like neckties, which they considered contrary to their testimony of simplicity.

J. WYLE

## Shuttered

c.1895, Alexander Street, Waterford

'House in Alexander Street', commissioned by W. McCoy shows a once fine establishment, now closed up, but still with lots of potential, and two resident corner boys to keep watch. Note the lack of shoes.

The public house was occupied by the Wyley family and one of the sons of the house, John J. Wyley would go on to become the Mayor of Waterford.

## Wild Man from Borneo

1895, Waterford

A.H. Poole captures a memorable image of half-bred Thoroughbred racehorse, 'Wild Man from Borneo'. Jockey and owner Tom Widger is seen holding the reins. Taken the same year that 'Wild Man' clinched victory in the Grand National, after coming third in the 1894 running.

CLYDE SHIPPIN

## *The Lizard*

c.1896, The Quay, Waterford

This photograph shows a jovial bunch both passengers and crew aboard *The Lizard* while docked at Waterford's quays.

Constructed by The Clyde Shipping Co. in Glasgow and launched in 1895, *The Lizard* was eventually sold to Turkey in 1925 and met its end in 1959.

## Baking the Blaa

c.1896, Adair's Bakehouse, Waterford

The rich, warm hues belie the image's age, evoking the tantalising aroma of freshly baked bread and batches of the famous Waterford 'blaa' (seen top middle). It's a scene that undoubtedly captures the ambiance of early morning at Mr Adair's Bakehouse at 18 Lady Lane and an age-old Waterford tradition, which has stood the test of time. Mr Adair was a prolific inventor with many patents to his name, one of which was for a baker's oven.

FATHER.MATTHEW
BOYS.BRIGADE

## Boys' Brigade

28 May 1898, The Quay, Waterford

The Father Mathews Boys' Brigade troop, visiting from the US, parade along the Quay with Emmet Fife and Drum Band in commemoration of the centenary of the 1798 Battle of Ross.

## *The Hansa*

1899, The Quay, Waterford

In November 1899 A.H. Poole captures the captain and first mate of *The Hansa*, a ship that unfortunately ran aground on Drumroe Bank near Duncannon, Co. Wexford. Poole likely journeyed with the rescue tugs to secure this onboard shot.

The source of *The Hansa* name began as a network of long-distance merchants and developed into a powerful association of cities: the Hanseatic League. For more than 400 years, the Hanseatic League shaped the economy, trade and politics of northern Europe.

# 1900–1930

## Suir Crossing

1914, Waterford

Bustling with horse-drawn carriages and passersby, Redmond Bridge spans the River Suir in Waterford city a year after its opening by John Redmond, M.P. and leader of the Irish Parliamentary Party. It would be replaced by Rice Bridge in 1986. Did you know that at the Redmond Bridge point, the River Suir is five times wider than the River Liffey at the O'Connell Bridge in Dublin?

## The Apple Seller

c.1900, The Apple Market, Waterford

Selling apples at the Apple Market is Margaret (Peggy) Roche, a charming Appleseller smoking her 'dudeen' clay pipe. Born in 1839, Peggy was the great grandmother of Hal Roche. No doctors anywhere near here with all these apples around!

## Opening Hunt Meet

c.1900, The Mall, Waterford

This gloriously dynamic shot by Poole captures crowds and horses assembled at The Imperial Hotel on The Mall for the opening meet of a fox hunt before heading for Ballinakill. The backdrop features Tower Lane, now part of The Tower Hotel.

J.D.WALSH
65

DENTIST
DENTIST

FRYS CHOCOLATE

## Arundel Square

c.1900, Arundel Square, Waterford

Arundel Square meets *A Christmas Carol* in this photo with a palpably Dickensian feel to it.

Shoppers mill around the square, named after the gate of the same name in the old city wall. Blurred busy figures thread the wet slabs from the Dominican foundation of 1226 seen in the centre, with the historic Blackfriars tower, dating from the fifteenth century, in the background.

## Downward Spiral

c.1900, Waterford

Lloyd's Circus presents a heart-stopping moment: a daredevil in the midst of a thrilling performance.

Regardless of the outcome, he certainly reached the bottom. A ray of sunlight highlights a portion of the entranced Waterford audience, emphasising the electric ambiance as the troupe journeyed through Ireland and Britain.

## Otter Hunt

14 May 1901, Curraghmore, Co. Waterford

Poole's lens captures the dynamism of the scene as an otter hunt commences at Curraghmore, near Portlaw. Despite the elegance displayed, the hunt's nature contrasts with modern sentiments bringing Oscar Wilde's famous quote to mind.

> 'The unspeakable in pursuit of the uneatable!'
>
> – Oscar Wilde

## *Sibyl*

c.1900, Cappoquin, Co. Waterford

A.H. Poole captures the paddle steamer *Sibyl*, poised for departure with passengers already onboard. The scene unfolds on the River Blackwater near Cappoquin.

## J. Knox is Dead

c.1901, Ballygunner, Co. Waterford

The funeral procession of J. Knox of Belvedere, Newtown took place at St Mary's in Ballygunner and was captured by A.H. Poole. Clergy, undertakers and mourners are present, women however are notably absent from the funeral procession, reflecting the custom of the time that it was a business to be left only to men to deal with.

## Ready. Steady. Go!

c.1901, People's Park, Waterford

A dramatic scene as cyclists prepare for a race at People's Park, on a track established a decade earlier by pioneer William G.D. Goff in 1891. The sport of cycling has a long tradition in Waterford city and county.

MACHINE PRINTING WORKS.
DUNGARVAN
POST OFFICE
CO HLAN

## Fair Day, Dungarvan

c.1902, Davitt Square, Dungarvan, Co. Waterford

Robert French vividly captures the bustling atmosphere of a fair day in Dungarvan. Cattle are aplenty, with eager sellers and buyers engaging in negotiations, and upon reaching a deal, signified by the traditional hand slapping.

## The First Cars

1901, The Mall, Waterford

This photograph shows a significant moment on The Mall in Waterford city. The bearded gentleman at the wheel is Waterford businessman and motoring pioneer, William G.D. Goff, driving his Daimler motor car. He was also the chairman of the Irish Automobile Club. Seated beside him, boasting impressive facial hair, is Col. McGrath, recognised as the first motorist in Wexford. To their right is RJ Mecredy, often referred to as 'The Father of Motoring in Ireland'.

Both Mecredy and Goff played pivotal roles in bringing the Motor Tour to Ireland in 1901. This photo was taken during the Great 1,000-Mile Irish Tour organised by the Irish Automobile Club.

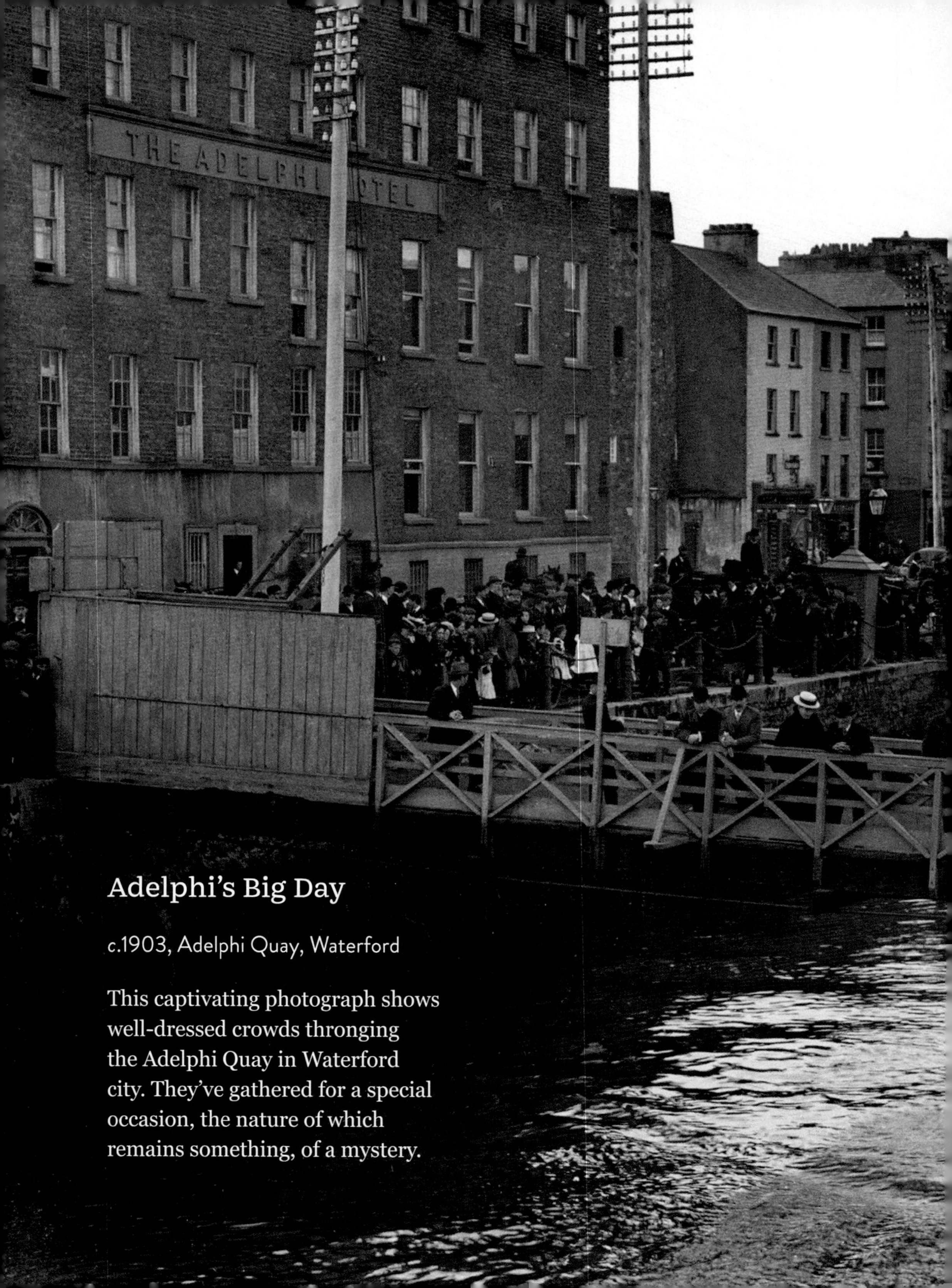


## Adelphi's Big Day

c.1903, Adelphi Quay, Waterford

This captivating photograph shows well-dressed crowds thronging the Adelphi Quay in Waterford city. They've gathered for a special occasion, the nature of which remains something, of a mystery.

BOVRIL
BOVRIL
BOVRIL
BOVRIL

## Chiseled Body of Men

1903, Waterside, Waterford

A group of stonemasons stand tall at Mr Costen's yard in Waterside. Many of the men proudly sport an ivy leaf, commemorating Ivy Day in honour of Charles Stewart Parnell, who had passed away roughly twelve years prior on 6 October 1891.

## Mia Farrow's Great-Uncle

2 May 1904, Poole Studio, Waterford

Edward Francis Frazer was born in China, but grew up in Ireland. He attend Aravon boarding school in Bray, Co. Wicklow. His Royal Field Artillery helmet crest and military records revealed that Edward served in Nigeria during World War I. He survived the war.

Edward was Maureen O'Sullivan's uncle. She is most famous for playing Jane opposite Johnny Weissmuller in all those black and white *Tarzan* films. Maureen was Mia Farrow's mother, which makes Edward, her great-uncle.

## The Royal Visit

1904, Grange Cove, Waterford

King Edward VII and Queen Alexandra graced Ireland's oldest city with their royal presence.

After an eventful visit, they departed from St Patrick's Park, Grange Cove, following the knighting of Mayor Councillor J.A. Power.

## Rockfield Players

c.1904, Tramore, Co. Waterford

A delightful ensemble of hockey players gather at Rockfield House on Church Road, Tramore, Co. Waterford.

This Poole photograph masterfully highlights the beauty of the group, complemented by a Humber bicycle partially visible in the backdrop.

## Infernal Machine

1905, Gracedieu, Waterford

On 29 August 1905 the construction of a new railway cutting in Gracedieu was in full swing. The scene presents a fascinating contrast between age-old methods, represented by the horse and the modern infernal machine.

W B C
W B C

## Waterford Boat Club

c.1906, Poole Studio, Waterford

Five esteemed members of the Waterford Boat Club proudly display their awards.

The gentleman seated on the left is Austin Farrell (1872–1934), who also appears in many other club photographs.

## Peerless De Wet

1906, Poole Studio, Waterford

Peerless de Wet, the celebrated greyhound and winner of the 1905 inaugural Irish Cup (showcased in the photograph), stands proudly. Born in 1902, he was owned by R.F. Phelan from Waterford, likely the gentleman on the right. The man on the left is P. O'Toole, the dog's trainer. The champion greyhound was named in honour of the legendary Boer General, Christiaan Rudolf de Wet.

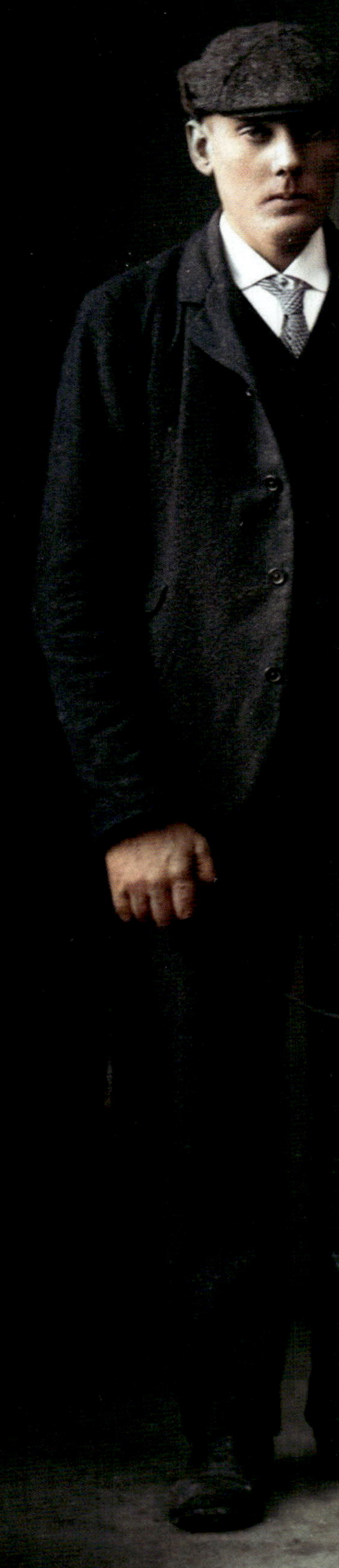

THE IRISH CUP
CLOHNANNA

## The Copper Coast

1906, Bunmahon, Co. Waterford

Copper miners stand atop precarious headstocks overlooking a new pit. The scene is accentuated by a winding wheel in the foreground and a winding house to the right, in Bunmahon, a renowned copper mining region in Co. Waterford.

## The Power of Love

1906, Dungarvan, Co. Waterford

Thomas Power, accompanied by his children and their dog, represents the Power family of Dungarvan, proprietors of Power's Blackwater Cider. The poignant gap in the centre of the photographs's composition pays tribute to Ellen Power, the family matriarch, who tragically had succumbed to tuberculosis just three months prior.

## Blackwater Cider

c.1906, Dungarvan, Co. Waterford

Mr T. Power, a cider manufacturer from Dungarvan, Co. Waterford, oversees the production of his famed Blackwater cider. A prominent figure of his era, he wore many hats: chairman of Waterford County Council, brewer, wine merchant, cider-maker, baker, jam-maker and politician.

## Hold a Candle

1906, Bunmahon, Co. Waterford

On Monday, 11 June 1906, Mr Meardon and his team ventured into the depths of the Bunmahon Mines, guided solely by the flicker of candlelight. This intimate underground snapshot highlights the stark contrast between the workers and the supervisors, the latter distinguished by their pristine white jackets.

DISPENSING DEPARTMENT

PERF
COD LIVER OIL
PAIN KILLER
MEDICAL
CLOTH CLEANER

## Jones Chemist

1907, The Quay, Waterford

Mr Jones' exquisitely appointed chemist shop stands at 82 The Quay. This highly detailed photograph reveals products like Oriental Toothpaste, Zox and Zam-Buk. Intriguingly, beneath the cod liver oil bottles are containers labelled 'Chemical Food!'

An advertisement for Barnet Bromide Photographic papers rests atop a camera, surrounded by darkroom supplies.

Tragically, Mr Jones would succumb to a self-administered drug overdose in 1931, at the age of fifty, 'while unsound of mind' as per records of his death.

## If the Suit Fits

25 July 1907, The Quay, Waterford

A wonderful photograph showing tailors hard at work in Hearne's at 63-64 The Quay. The central figure's confident stance leaves no doubt about who's in charge. The tailor on the middle right appears lost in thought, perhaps dreaming of distant lands.

Tailors traditionally worked seated on the floor, cross-legged, with their work draped over their laps. In French, this pose is still referred to as '*Assis en Tailleur*' or 'sitting tailor-style'.

## Fore(!) in Tramore

18 September 1907, Tramore, Co. Waterford

Mr Clampett and Mr Downes, accompanied by their young caddies, are engrossed in a game at Tramore golf links. The expressions on the boys' faces are priceless, with Brownstown head visible in the distance.

## Lieutenant Becher

1908, Lismore, Co. Waterford

Edmund Becher, aged eleven, was the cherished son of Edmund W. and Ella Becher of Ardagh, Lismore. Tragically, just eight years after this photograph, Lieutenant Edmund Becher would fall in battle at the age of nineteen while serving with the Royal Munster Fusiliers in France, 1916.

A tribute from Ireland's Roll of Honour in *The Irish Times*, 23 December 1916, commemorates his bravery and potential:

> Mr Edward W. Becher, Castlefarm House, Lismore, whose only son, Sec. Lieut. E. R. F. Becher, Royal Munster Fusiliers, recently died from wounds received in action, has received a letter from Major-General Hickie, conveying his sincere sympathy. Lieutenant Becher, he said, had already been brought to his notice for gallant conduct and skilful leadership, and had he survived he would have been recommended for the Military Cross … expressing the sorrow of all ranks in the Munster Fusiliers, and bearing testimony to Lieutenant Becher's gallantry, untiring energy, keenness, and courage.

MILFORD HOTEL

## The Royal

1908, Lombard Street, Waterford

The Royal Hotel, formerly known as the Milford Hotel, undergoes renovations on a corner near Lombard Street. The precarious scaffolding, hoist and the presence of workers (including a child) at the top would surely raise eyebrows today among health and safety inspectors. The lone ladder reaching the summit seems like a daunting climb, especially on a gusty day.

## *Dartmouth Castle*

c.1908, Cappoquin, Co. Waterford

Around 1908, the *Dartmouth Castle* is seen embarking passengers for what no doubt would have been a fine pleasure cruise at Cappoquin in County Waterford. Note: the array of fancy hats.

DARTMOUTH CASTLE

## Fitzgerald Family

1909, Waterford Castle, The Island

The esteemed Fitzgerald family stands proudly at the entrance of their residence, Waterford Castle, situated on The Island in the River Suir. The Fitzgerald lineage has been intertwined with the island's history since the twelfth century.

THE HOME AND COLONIAL
Home and Colonial Stores Limited
FINEST
BUTTER 1/-
HOME AND COLONIAL
NOW ONLY

## Colonial Home

1910, Broad Street, Waterford

An impressive line up of shop assistants proudly stand outside The Home and Colonial Stores Limited on Broad Street. The elegant shop window showcases an array of tea packets and a placard prominently advertises: 'Finest Irish Creamery Butter 1/- (No Higher Price).'

## Eviction!

1910, O'Connell Street, Waterford

While the crowd soak up the excitement of the scene with police and a photographer present, the girl in the first-floor window holds her puppy while looking down mournfully upon her possessions, piled up at the side of O'Connell Street below.

CTIONEER

## Freemasons

21 October 1910, The Mall, Waterford

A gathering of the branches of the Masonic Order convened in Waterford. This photograph, likely taken from Poole Studio's rear window, showcases members from the Craft, Royal Arch, Preceptory, and Rose Croix freemasons.

R.W. Bro. Andrews is seated in middle of the front row with his hands crossed on his lap.

## Life Savers

1910, Tramore, Co. Waterford

Lifeboat crew pictured with their boat *Henley*, named in honour of its benefactor, Mrs G. Henley of Highbury. Serving Tramore from 1893 to 1918, this vessel played a crucial role in rescuing nineteen lives during its tenure.

## Dr Mary Strangman

c.1910, Poole Studio, Waterford

A portrait of Dr Mary Somerville Parker Strangman, a physician, public health advocate, botanist, suffragette and Waterford's first female Councillor, elected in 1912.

Born in Carriganore, Killotteran, Strangman established her Waterford practice in 1903 while volunteering with local women's charities where she conducted pioneering work in treating alcoholism and morphine addictions. She published a number of articles on the subject, one of which was entitled 'Morphinomania treated successfully with atrophine, strychnine.'

Her contributions to medicine and society echo to this day.

## High Sheriff of Waterford

18 February 1911, Cappoquin, Co. Waterford

In this fetching photograph Sir Richard John Musgrave, 5th Baronet of Tourin (1850–1930), is seen enjoying a moment with his Jack Russell terrier.

Once the High Sheriff of County Waterford in 1880, this candid shot offers a glimpse into life at his Cappoquin residence.

## Redmond Elected

1910, O'Connell Street, Waterford

The scene inside the Waterford Court House, as a crowd gathers for the nomination of John Redmond, M.P. Notably, Redmond himself is absent from the photograph.

& SOUTH EASTERN RAILWAY

## Tramore Harriers

March 1912, O'Connell Street, Waterford

The Tramore Harriers assemble at The Mall in Waterford. This vibrant scene, captured by Poole, is filled with activity. This image was taken just a month prior to the sinking of the *Titanic*.

## Rosamond Jacob

1912, Poole Studio, Waterford

This striking image captures Rosamond Jacob, a prominent Waterford native born in 1888 on South Parade, Newtown, Waterford city.

A multifaceted figure, Jacob was an Irish suffragist, republican, socialist, author and social activist. Her influence extended throughout Waterford, and in 1914, she played a key role in establishing the first Waterford Cumann na mBan branch.

Her series of diaries, filled with keen observations, provide valuable insights into the aftermath of the 1916 Rising. Her legacy as a feminist and nationalist continues to resonate in Irish history.

## Daddy Long-Legs

1913, Waterford

Olympic gold medalist and world-record long jumper Peter O'Connor is captured here with his wife, Margaret, and six of their children (they eventually had nine).

A founding member and vice-president of Waterford Athletic Club, O'Connor's legacy in the sport is still remembered. He passed away in Waterford on 9 November 1957.

## Ada's Bouquet

1914, Poole Studio, Waterford

This is a striking image of Ada, John Redmond's wife, holding her bouquet. She's accompanied by a large group of ladies. The photograph boasts one of the finest displays of early twentieth-century ladies' millinery.

These formidable women exude an air of authority; they look as though they could run not just a small country, but any nation, and still break for tea at 4 o'clock! Notably, several ladies are adorned with Ancient Order of Hibernian badges.

WIRELESS
ARNOLD

## Marconi Room

14 March 1914, Custom House Quay, Waterford

A glimpse into the Marconi Room in one of Waterford's steamship offices, likely the Clyde Shipping Company offices at Custom House Quay.

This fascinating snapshot offers a behind-the-scenes look at early twentieth-century communications, with 'Wireless World' prominently displayed. The young operator, captured in this moment, could never have foreseen what 'wireless' technology would become within a hundred years of this photograph being taken.

## Fethard Lifeboat Disaster

1914, The Quay, Waterford

These are the crew members of a Norwegian vessel who survived the Fethard lifeboat disaster. *The Mexico*, carrying a cargo of mahogany and cedar from Mexico, ran aground on the Keeragh Islands, Co. Wexford on Friday, 20 February 1914.

The sailor in the middle is believed to be the captain of *The Mexico*, Ole Edvin Eriksen, of Fredrikshald, Norway. Their survival stands as a testament to resilience and fortitude in the face of maritime peril.

59
63

## Torpedos Away!

c.1914, The Quay, Waterford

British Navy torpedo boats docked at the Quays. Likely taking part in wargames that took place every few years, around the end of the nineteenth and beginning of twentieth century, off the coasts of Ireland and Britain. Identifiable are H.M. Torpedo Boats 49, 59, 63 – launched 1886, decommissioned in 1919, 1913 and 1919 respectively (59 and 63 were sold).

## Horsemen and Marshals

1914, The Court House, Waterford

The organisers and stewards for a Redmondite Home Rule rally in Waterford. Standing and posing for their moment in time, the horsemen were responsible for keeping back the swelling crowds. Equipped with a loud-hailer for crowd management, they maintained order during this significant political event.

## Miss Hookey's Team

1915, The Court House, Waterford

This photograph captures Miss Monica Hookey of 1 Bank Lane, Waterford, alongside her spirited camogie team. Seated on the ground to the left is Monica Hookey, who later passed away in Welling, Kent, in 1977. The image was taken at the rear of Waterford Court House, preserving a moment of camaraderie and athletic pride.

## Con Colbert

c.1915, Poole Studio, Waterford

Con Colbert, seated to the right, was the captain of F Company of the Fourth Battalion. He was in command at the Marrowbone Lane distillery when it was surrendered during the Easter Rising.

His execution took place on 8 May 1916, alongside Seán Heuston, Michael Mallin and Éamonn Ceannt.

## Shamrocks

1916, Ferrybank, Waterford

A triumphant moment for the Shamrock Hurling Club of Ferrybank, captured in all their glory. They secured back-to-back Waterford County titles in 1915–1916, defeating Young Ireland in a replay by 5 goals to 3-3.

The team members included T. McElroy, J. Norris, T. Morrissey (Captain), T. Henebry, T. Heffernan, W. Murphy, J. O'Meara, P. Freeman, W. Bell, J. Brett, M. Barron, M. O'Brien, P. Fitzpatrick, J. Treacy and P. Fitzpatrick.

HECTOR
SHAMP
WAT
CO. CH
19

FEEHAN
RODNEY
H.C.
FORD
PIONS
16.

J. M
5

ORGAN
THE

## J. Morgan's

25 February 1916, Broad Street, Waterford

A proud moment for the staff of J. Morgan's butcher shop, captured as they stand before an impressive display of mutton, beef and pork on Broad Street.

The man front and centre, likely Mr Morgan himself, is distinguished by his butchering belt, symbolising his craft and expertise.

## The Countess in Waterford

c.1917, Poole Studio, Waterford

A significant moment captured in Waterford, featuring Countess Constance Markievicz, her dog, Poppet, Thomas McDonald and Theobald Wolfe Tone Fitzgerald in the Poole Studio. The Countess, a key figure in Irish history, gave lectures on the 1916 Rising at Waterford city Hall, sharing her insights and experiences with the local community.

Her presence in Waterford, along with her companions, stands as a testament to the enduring connection between national figures and local communities during a pivotal time in Ireland's history.

## The Wolfhound of Waterford

21 February 1917, Waterford

A drummer boy from the Band of the Irish Guards is photographed at Waterford Barracks, accompanied by regiment's regal mascot –a nine-year-old Wolfhound named Leitrim Boy.

## Happy Glampers

11 July 1918, Tramore, Co. Waterford

Mr Thomas Foley, originally of Manor Street, and Johanna Hartnett, originally of Grand Hotel, Tramore, are captured enjoying a camping holiday in Tramore with their dog in front of a pretty wooden compact caravan. The photo offers a glimpse into their leisure time away from their home in Sweetbriar Terrace, Waterford city.

## William Redmond

18 March 1918, Poole Studio, Waterford

William Archer Redmond (1886–1932). A significant political figure, Redmond served as MP in the House of Commons of the United Kingdom of Great Britain and Ireland, and later as a Teachta Dála (TD) in Dáil Éireann. He is one of the rare individuals to have served in both political bodies.

Redmond is seen wearing a black armband, likely in mourning for his recently deceased father, John Redmond, who led the Irish Parliamentary Party (1900–1918).

## Déise Dev

20 March 1918, Poole Studio, Waterford

Éamon de Valera, MP for East Clare, captured by Poole at his studio.

Notably, de Valera is wearing the Fáinne (the Irish word for ring), a symbol signifying an Irish speaker.

He was present in Waterford to rally support for his party, particularly as there was likely a political vacuum in the area following John Redmond's death on 6 March 1918. As just noted, John Redmond was leader of the Irish Parliamentary Party.

## Mayor Vincent White

29 February 1920, Poole Studio, Waterford

This photograph features Dr Vincent White adorned in his Mayoral robes and Chain of Office. Dr White holds the distinction of being the first Sinn Féin Mayor of Waterford, serving from 1920–1926.

## Michael Staines

1918, Poole Studio, Waterford

Michael Staines pictured in Poole's Studio, was prominent in Irish history. A member of the Irish Republican Brotherhood (IRB), part of its Supreme Council (1921–1922), he served as quartermaster of the General Post Office garrison during the 1916 Rising.

His influence extended into law enforcement, as he went on to become the first commissioner of An Garda Síochána.

## Wacky Races

26 June 1920, Tramore, Co. Waterford

A lively snapshot of the O'Gorman Bros. Social Club, lined up with an impressive array of Humber, Austin and Chevrolet cars at Tramore Railway Station. Captured by Poole, this spirited group appears poised for adventure and good times on the road, embodying the joy and camaraderie of the era.

## Plane Lucky

November 1920, Barrack Street, Waterford

A dramatic scene unfolds as a 'Scout' plane, tasked with carrying despatches from Fermoy to Waterford Barracks, crashes into the roofs of two houses opposite the Barracks. The plane, flown by the lucky flying officers Briggs and McKiehan, escaped with a broken leg and arm respectively and narrowly missed causing a catastrophe.

The house on the left belonged to Mr Aspel's licensed premises, while the house on the right was privately owned by Mrs McSweeney.

## De La Salle

9 June 1920, De La Salle College, Newtown, Waterford

A proud display of Hurling heritage in this photograph of the De La Salle Hurling team. Each player's county is inscribed on his hurley, representing Corcaigh (Cork), Gaillimhe (Galway), Cill Chainnigh (Kilkenny), Tiobraid Árann (Tipperary) and Luimneach (Limerick). The captain, holding the sliothair, represents An Clár (Clare).

Two men in the photo are marked with Waterford club names, though their specific identities remain unknown.

H 1490
L. ASPEL
29
LICENSED

SOCIAL CLUB
HI·78

SOCIAL CLUB
Austin
HI 273
HI·T2

Corcaig
Gaillimh
CORCAIG
CORCAIG Abú
Corcaig Abú
Tiobraid Árann
Corcaig
Cláir Abú!
1920
Tiobraid Árann
Luimneach

Cill Coinniġ
Cill Coinniġ
Cill Coinniġ
Luimneaċ Abú

## Top Hats Trilbys and Bowlers

24 February 1922, Tramore, Co. Waterford

A fashionable assembly of top hats, trilbys and bowlers mark the occasion of Cornelius Phelan's marriage to Bridget Walsh in Tramore. Bridget was the niece of Canon Nicholas Walsh, the parish priest of Tramore at the time.

## Lacey's Public House

22 November 1922, Johnstown, Waterford

Lacey's Public House in Johnstown, Waterford looking like it's seen better days in this photograph. Later owned by legendary hurler Philly Grimes, the establishment's facade tells a story of its own. An advertisement for Downses is visible in the window, and next door, a touching scene as a little boy is minded by his big sister.

PALE
ALE

GRANVILLE HOTEL
64
& CO. LTD
GRANVILLE
HEARNE & CO

HEARNE & C°
LIMITED.
63
62

## The Granville

July 1922, The Quay, Waterford

This poignant photograph, taken between 18 and 20 July 1922, captures a moment of significant upheaval during the Irish Civil War. Featuring two of Waterford's iconic establishments, Hearnes Shop and the Granville Hotel (the birthplace of Thomas Francis Meagher), the image is a stark reminder of the city's turbulent past.

During the Free State offensive on Waterford, many citizens evacuated the city to escape four days of intense fighting. Tragically, five civilians were still killed in the shelling and crossfire.

## Gracedieu

27 September 1923, Gracedieu, Co. Waterford

This intriguing photograph captures a farm under the watchful eye of Free State soldiers, taken just four months after the official end of the Irish Civil War. The presence of the armed guard raises questions and adds a layer of complexity to the image.

THE CORNER HOUS
E&C. WILLCOCKS
CANADA & USA

GLADSTONE
STREET
THE CORNER HOUSE

## Gladstone Street Corner

1924, Gladstone St, Waterford

A bustling corner house and shop at the intersection of Gladstone Street and Great George's Street in Waterford city. The display showcases a diverse array of goods, reflecting the commerce of the time.

## Ferryboat

c.1920s, Dungarvan, Co. Waterford

Some very dapper looking passengers on a ferryboat off Dungarvan Harbour. Maybe going to or returning from Sunday Mass. This photograph is from the personal papers of Fr Nessan Shaw OFM Cap. (1915–1997), a Capuchin friar and native of Dungarvan.

&
Hosiery
JOHN B
BREN
Horrockses FLANNELETTES
Horrockses FLANNELETTES
HORROCKSES
IDEAL FABRIC
Horrockses' SHEETS & PILLOW CASES
We stock Horrockses FLANNELETTES
Horrockses FLANNELETTES
BRENNAN

ENNAN
PRINTED VOILES
DIAPHALENE
Quite New
Horrockses
Latest Style
1/6
OVERALL CLOTH
SATEENS SATINS
We stock
Horrockses
OVERALL CLOTHS
OVERALL CLOTHS
BRENNAN

## Brennan's

10 May 1926, Barronstrand Street, Waterford

A cheerful moment captured at Brennan's drapery & hosiery shop at 27 Barronstrand Street, Waterford.

Mr John Brennan and his son James Michael stand proudly in the doorway, surrounded by windows showcasing Horrockses, Voile, Diaphalene, and dainty lingerie.

## A Civil Welcome

20 August 1928, City Hall, Waterford

The Lord Mayor of Waterford and owner of the *Munster Express*, Edward Walsh, extended a warm civic welcome to Father Walsh, a priest (possibly related) who was visiting the city.

## St Patrick's Day Committee

1927, Poole Studio, Waterford

A formal portrait of Mayor John J. Wyley, aged thirty-five, alongside the Waterford Saint Patrick's Day organising committee of 1927. A glimpse into the civic pride and community spirit of the era.

## Patricia

1929, Coal Quay, Waterford

Patricia Kelly's hairdressing salon at No. 94 Coal Quay, featuring a range of hair products from the time, presumably she's the young woman pictured in the middle. The shop is now called 'Shoobaloo'.

94
HIGH CLASS LADIES &
GENTS HAIRDRESSING.
P
DULCIA

cia"
HIGH GLASS LADIES &
GENTS HAIRDRESSING.
94
P

# *Gone to Tramore*

On Saturday, 17 November 1928 Arthur Henri Poole left a note for his dear wife, Elizabeth, that simply read: 'Gone to Tramore ... may stay overnight'. Inexplicably and tragically, he never returned home and the great photographer was lost and never seen again.

A week later, the *Waterford Standard* newspaper of Saturday, 24 November 1928 reported on his disappearance and appealed, in vain, for information about his whereabouts:

**MR. A. H. POOLE MISSING.**

Mr. A. H. Poole, The Mall, Waterford, has been missing from home for the past week.

On Friday, 16th inst., he left home shortly after 8 o'clock. He left a note saying that he was going to Tramore, and that he might remain there for the night.

On Saturday, as he did not return, the Civic Guards were notified by members of his family.

Up to the present Mr. Poole has not returned, and his family would be glad of any information as to his whereabouts.

• • •

Arthur was declared legally dead at inquest in 1931 and the Pooles continued to run the family business following his disappearance up to the 1950s, preserving the legacy of a great photographer whose work continues to captivate and inspire.

# 1930–1962

## Snow Angel

16 December 1929, The Courthouse, Waterford

A festive photograph, taken outside Waterford Courthouse, captures a delightful moment from the winter season. A wagon filled with Christmas trees from William Power Seed Merchants on O'Connell Street. The little girl snow angel is a daughter of the Power family. She seems pretty content with herself; the same cannot be said for the fella leading the horse who looks like he'd rather be home eating the turkey.

## Wood Nymphs

2 September, 1930, Kilmeaden, Co. Waterford

This enchanting photograph captures a group of young girls dressed as fairies or wood nymphs. They were rehearsing for a charity fundraising performance, organised by Lady Irene Graham of Mount Congreve, Kilmeaden.

## Adele Astaire

1932, Lismore, Co. Waterford

Adele Astaire with her husband, Lord Charles Arthur Francis Cavendish, pictured at their home, Lismore Castle, Co. Waterford. The American dancer, stage actress and singer built a successful performance career with her younger brother Fred Astaire.

Fred was widely regarded as the 'greatest popular-music dancer of all time'. He also had a longstanding relationship to Lismore, visiting the area from the mid-1930s until well into the 1970s.

## Saints and Sinners

1932, St John of God NS, Waterford

In this wonderful photograph by Poole, we see a delightful line up of children dressed as little angels and devils for a play at St John of God Girls' National School in Waterford. Saint Patrick certainly has pride of place in this tableau amid a really great mix of expressions on view.

EXCELLER
EXTRA SPECIAL

## Bishop Foy School

23 June 1932, Parnell St, Waterford

Established in the late 1600s and closed in 1967, this photograph shows a cricket team of well-dressed young men, some looking serious; others bored, all surely destined for great things. Given the date, it's likely that some may may later be involved in WWII.

## How the Sausage is Made!

24 September 1937, Morgan St, Waterford

A beautifully lit shot showing the sausage-making room of Messrs H. Denny Factory, Morgan Street, Waterford city. The image showcases an iconic Avery scales, an old-fashioned lineshaft powering machinery through leather belts and small electric motors driving high-speed machines.

# H. Downes & Co.

October 1936, Thomas Street, Waterford

An industrious scene showing the cellar at Henry Downes & Co. with staff working away. The barrels, one of which is being tapped, were filled with Choice Old Port, Fined.

Henry Downes was established in 1797 on Thomas Street. An unsung piece of living memory and a well-hidden part of Waterford's merchant and social history.

DOWNES & Co
WATERFORD

## Breaking News!

29 July 1938, O'Connell Street, Waterford

A row of typesetters captured working intently on linotype machines at *The Waterford News*. Amid the controlled chaos, the image conveys the urgency of a looming deadline. Established in 1848, the newspaper continues to thrive today as the *Waterford News & Star*.

## Packing Power

13 November 1942, O'Connell Street, Waterford

This scene takes us upstairs to the packing department of William Power & Co. Seed Merchants, located at 26 O'Connell Street. Now called Seedtech, the company was established in 1859 and to this day remains a family business.

## Wedding Bells

c.1946, Poole Studio, Waterford

A joyous wedding portrait of James O'Connell (Swansea) and Margaret McCormack (7 Sallypark) captured at the renowned Poole Studio. Their radiant smiles hint at the promise of a beautiful day and a fulfilling life together.

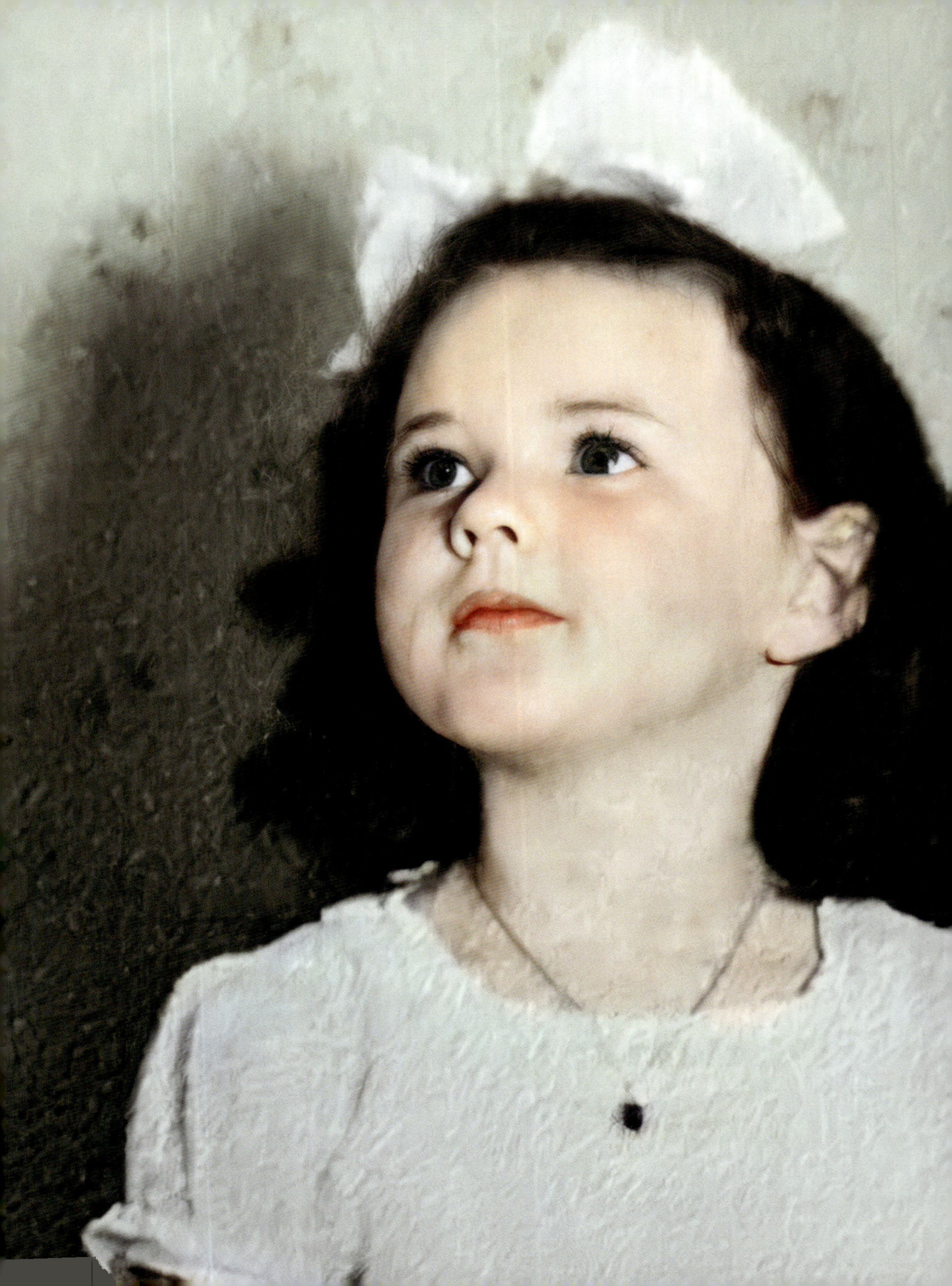

## Ryan's Daughter

c.1950s, Cork Road, Waterford

A slightly younger portrait of my mother, Eileen Ryan, daughter of Jackie and Joan Ryan of the Cork Road, Waterford city. Eileen was about five years of age when the photograph was taken by her uncle Joe O'Neill. Doesn't she look a lot like Shirley Temple? Even better I should say.

## Fiddler at the Fleadh

1957, Dungarvan, Co. Waterford

Fiddler at the Fleadh Cheoil. A warm scene of *craic agus ceol* featuring Dinny O'Brien, traditional fiddler as he entertains the crowd at the 1957 Fleadh Cheoil in Dungarvan.

## Large Bottle off the Shelf

c.1950s, Abbeyside Dungarvan, Co. Waterford

Relaxing with a large bottle off the shelf (but note the small glass), Tom Brett and John Hayes enjoy a moment of recreation. The large bottle is a must, and Tom was famously known to debate this simple fact of life with anyone who dared to challenge it.

## Heroes of '59

c.1959, Annie Brophy Studio, Waterford

1959 All-Ireland Senior Hurling Championship winners captured by Annie Brophy. Larry Guinan and Frankie Walsh pose with the McCarthy cup and a fine selection of silverware.

The famous image colourised incredibly well, went viral on social media and subsequently featured, along with an interview, in *The Irish Examiner* and *The Irish Times*.

Déise Abú!

ICHAEL
CAHILL

## Showband Joy

1961, Tramore, Co. Waterford

Derek Joy's Showband started life as the Swing Beats in Waterford city in early 1961. Like so many other bands, they were a local pop group who played at dances and performed concerts. Most of the band members were employees of the Waterford Glass factory.

The lineup in April 1961 included: Derek Joy (vocals), Jackie Power (guitar), Jimmy Foley (leader and guitar), Michael Cahill (drums), Tony O'Keeffe (keyboards), Edmond Walsh (sax), Nicholas Cahill (trumpet) and Noel Cahill (trombone). The three Cahills were brothers.

On 20 July 1962 the band would share the stage with American star Emile Ford and his Checkmates in a double bill gig in the Atlantic Ballroom in Tramore.

## Two Cool Dudes

1962, Olympia Ballroom, Waterford

This image is a very personal one, this photograph features Jim 'Jumbo' Lane with my father, Jimmy Hannigan, at the Olympia Ballroom at the height of the Showband era. Don't they look very dapper in their suits? For me, personally, it's fascinating to think that my parents hadn't even met when this photo was taken and I wasn't even a (colourised) twinkle in my father's eye. I dedicate this book to my family.

## The Poole Collection

A. H. Poole was a professional photographer who lived and worked in Waterford, from the late nineteenth century to the early twentieth century. He operated the A. H. Poole Studio, which was active from around 1884 to 1954. Poole's photographic works primarily captured the life and events in the Waterford area during that period. His collection includes photographs of local people, social events, sports, businesses, and various scenes of everyday life.

A large collection of Poole's photographs has been preserved by the National Library of Ireland, which has made them available online as a valuable historical resource.

While Poole's work is primarily focused on documenting daily life in Waterford, his photographs have gained international significance as a valuable historical record of Ireland in the late nineteenth and early twentieth centuries. Poole's photographs provide a unique insight into the people, culture and landscape of Ireland during this time. His images have been used by historians, researchers and scholars around the world as a way to provide a richer understanding of Irish history and culture at that time.

In particular, Poole's photographs have been used to study the social and economic changes that occurred in Ireland during this period, including the impact of the Irish War of Independence and the partition of Ireland. They have also been used to explore the history of photography in Ireland and the role of photography in shaping national identity.

Overall, while Poole's work is primarily focused on Waterford and the south-east of Ireland, its significance extends far beyond and has made a valuable contribution to the understanding of Irish history and culture on an international level.

Arthur Henri Poole was one of the most significant and skilled photographers of his time in Ireland. His work captures the people, culture and landscapes of Waterford and its surrounds in remarkable detail, and provides an invaluable record of life in the city during a period of revolutionary change.

Poole Collection on Tour, 1888

POOLE. WATERFORD
POOLE & Co.
11. MALL.
WATERFORD
SPECIALITIES
PHOTOGRAPHS

## Other Photographic and Archival Collections

### Lawrence Collection

The Lawrence Collection, held by the National Library of Ireland, comprises approximately 40,000 glass plate negatives that date from the 1870s to 1914. This extensive archive, created by the Dublin-based William Lawrence Photographic Studios, primarily features topographical images that document urban and rural landscapes, streetscapes, and notable buildings across Ireland. The photographs, many of which were taken by Robert French, provide a comprehensive visual record of Irish life during a period of significant social and economic transformation.

### Eblana Collection

The Eblana Photograph Collection consists of topographical views of Ireland, including cities, towns and rural areas. Also included are eviction scenes from the 1880s.

### The Breslin Archive

Established in 2019 by Irish educator, engineer and entrepreneur, professor John Breslin. The aim of the Breslin Archive is to digitally preserve analogue photographs of Ireland from the late nineteenth and early twentieth centuries. The Poole Collection, held by the Breslin Archive, is believed to be the work of The Poole Studio, Waterford. The collection comprises photographs taken during the 1890s of people, stately homes, houses, fishing ports and landscapes, mainly in County Waterford.

### Capuchin Order Ireland Archive

The archives contain the records of the Order of Friars Minor Capuchin in Ireland from 1615 to circa 1980, with the bulk of the papers relating to individual Capuchin Franciscans, Capuchin administration in the Irish province, sermon and retreat notes, and records relating to various lay sodalities and confraternities.

### Waterford County Museum

Waterford County Museum located in Dungarvan is dedicated to preserving and promoting the history of the locality. The museum is operational largely through voluntary effort and relies on the generosity of the public – both financially and in the donation of artefacts.

### The Irish Traditional Music Archive (ITMA)

ITMA is home to the largest, most comprehensive collection of Irish traditional music, song and dance in the world. ITMA's mission is to be the national public archive and resource centre for Irish traditional music, song and dance, and the globally-recognised specialist advisory agency to advance appreciation, knowledge, and the practice of Irish traditional music.

### Waterford City and County Archive

Waterford City and County Archives Service is an amalgamation of the City Archives in High Street, Waterford, and the County Archives in Dungarvan Library. The archive holds the records of local authorities in Waterford city and county, past and present and private collections relating to the city and county.

## References


### Books and Publications

*A Century of Trade and Enterprise in Waterford, Photographic Essay 1880's–1980's*, Bill Irish and Andrew Kelly, in Association with Waterford Civic Trust, 2009.

*Shadows of the Past: a photographic stroll through old Waterford*, Waterford civic trust and Waterford Musuem of Treasures, The Heritage Council, 2005.

*Waterford Streets Past and Present*, Daniel Dowling, Waterford Corporation, 1998.

*Waterford through the Lens of Time*, Jack O'Neill, self-published, 2009.

### Websites and Databases

National Library of Ireland
Catalogue National Library of Ireland Flickr Archive National Archives of Ireland
*Waterford News & Star* Waterford *Munster Express*
Waterford County Museum
Waterford Civic Trust
The Museum of Childhood Ireland
Dictionary of Irish Biography
*The Irish Times*
*The Irish Independent*
Wikimedia Commons

# Photographers and Sources

*Cover images*

**THE CLOCK TOWER**; Photographer: William Lawrence; Source: National Library of Ireland Eblana Ref.: EB_0918. **DROMANA GATE AND BRIDGE**; Photographer: Robert French; Source: National Library of Ireland Lawrence Ref.: L_CAB_00690.

*Opening Credits*

***THE SS PEMBROKE***; Photographer: Poole Studio; Source: National Library of Ireland Ref.: POOLEWP 1026. **BAKING THE BLAA**; Photographer: Poole Studio; Source: National Library of Ireland Ref.: POOLEWP 0111. **WOMAN AND DONKEY**; Photographer: Poole Studio; Source: National Library of Ireland Ref.: POOLEWP 3520. **JIM WARE**; Photographer: Annie Brophy; Source: Waterford City Archives / Waterford Treasures nan Ref.: nan.

*Waterford City and County, Colourisation and Restoration*

**REGINALDS TOWER**; Photographer: Robert French; Source: National Library of Ireland Ref.: L_ROY_02089. **APPLE MARKET BOYS**; Photographer: Poole Studio; Source: National Library of Ireland Ref.: POOLEWP 0293a.

*1840–1880*

**YOUNG IRELANDERS UNDER ARREST**; Photographer: Leone Glukman; Source: Wikimedia Commons nan Ref.: nan. **AN GORTA MÓR**; Photographer: John Gregory Crace; Source: Wikimedia Commons Sean Sexton Ref.: nan. **THOMAS FRANCIS MEAGHER**; Photographer: Mathew Benjamin Bray; Source: Wikimedia Commons NARA College Park collection Ref.: NWDNS- 111-B-5252. **THE CLOCK TOWER**; Photographer: William Lawrence; Source: National Library of Ireland Eblana Ref.: EB_0918. **DROMANA GATE**; Photographer: Robert French; Source: National Library of Ireland Lawrence Ref.: L_CAB_00690. **THE SQUARE**; Photographer: Robert French; Source: National Library of Ireland Lawrence Ref.: L_CAB_04057.

*1880–1900*

**THE DRAPER'S WIFE**; Photographer: Poole Studio; Source: National Library of Ireland Ref.: POOLEWP 0153. **ASYLUM**; Photographer: Poole Studio; Source: National Library of Ireland Ref.: POOLEWP 0131. **DAN FRAHER**; Photographer: Edmund Keohan; Source: Waterford County Museum nan Ref.: EK1687. **LAFCADIO HEARN**; Photographer: Unknown; Source: Wikimedia Commons Ref.: N/A. **BROAD STREET**; Photographer: Robert French; Source: National Library of Ireland Lawrence Ref.: L_ROY_03078. **THE MALL**; Photographer: Robert French; Source: National Library of Ireland Lawrence Ref.: L_CAB_00244. **DUNMORE PIER**; Photographer: Poole Studio; Source: The Breslin Archive Ref.: N/A. **BALLYBRICKEN FAIR DAY**; Photographer: Poole Studio; Source: National Library of Ireland Ref.: POOLEIMP 515. **ALIVE, ALIVE-O!**; Photographer: Unknown; Source: Andy Kelly Ref.: N/A. **THE MEN'S SLIP**; Photographer: Robert French; Source: National Library of Ireland Lawrence Ref.: L_ROY_09090. **COCKLE PICKERS**; Photographer: Poole Studio; Source: National Library of Ireland Ref.: POOLEWP 3522. **THE POOLE FAMILY**; Photographer: Poole Studio; Source: National Library of Ireland Ref.: POOLEWP 1000. **BATHING BOX LADY**; Photographer: Unknown; Source: A Century of Enterprise and Trade Jack O'Neil/Bill Irish Ref.: N/A. **THE BELLS**; Photographer: Poole Studio; Source: National Library of Ireland Ref.: POOLEWP. **SHUTTERED**; Photographer: Poole Studio; Source: National Library of Ireland Ref.: POOLEWP 0687. **WILD MAN FROM BORNEO**; Photographer: Poole Studio; Source: National Library of Ireland Ref.: POOLEIMP 345A. ***THE LIZARD***; Photographer: Poole Studio; Source: National Library of Ireland Ref.: POOLEWP 0971a. **BAKING THE BLAA**; Photographer: Poole Studio; Source: National Library of Ireland Ref.: POOLEWP 0111. **BOYS' BRIGADE**; Photographer: Poole Studio; Source: National Library of Ireland Ref.: POOLEWP 0956. ***THE HANSA***; Photographer: Poole Studio; Source: National Library of Ireland Ref.: POOLEWP 1096.

*1900–1930*

**SUIR CROSSING**; Photographer: Robert French; Source: National Library of Ireland Lawrence Ref.: L_ROY_11509. **THE APPLE SELLER**; Photographer: Unknown; Source: National Library of Ireland Jack O'Neill Ref.: N/A. **OPENING HUNT MEET**; Photographer: Poole Studio; Source: National Library of Ireland Ref.: POOLEWP 0265a. **ARUNDEL SQUARE**; Photographer: Poole Studio; Source: National Library of Ireland Ref.: POOLEWP 0527a. **DOWNWARD SPIRAL**; Photographer: Poole Studio; Source: National Library of Ireland Ref.: POOLEWP 0912. **OTTER HUNT**; Photographer: Poole Studio; Source: National Library of Ireland Ref.: POOLEWP 0334. ***SIBYL***; Photographer: Robert French; Source: National Library of Ireland Lawrence Ref.: L_CAB_05845. **J. KNOX IS DEAD**; Photographer: Poole Studio; Source: National Library of Ireland Ref.: POOLEWP 1230. **READY. STEADY. GO!**; Photographer: Poole Studio; Source: National Library of Ireland Ref.: POOLEWP 0345. **FAIR DAY, DUNGARVAN**; Photographer: Robert French; Source: National Library of Ireland Lawrence Ref.: L_ROY_03583. **THE FIRST CARS**; Photographer: Poole Studio; Source: National Library of Ireland Ref.: POOLEWP 0344. **ADELPHI'S BIG DAY**; Photographer: Poole Studio; Source: National Library of Ireland Ref.: POOLEWP 1311. **CHISELED BODY OF MEN**; Photographer: Poole Studio; Source: National Library of Ireland Ref.: POOLEWP 1309. **MIA FARROWS GREAT-UNCLE**; Photographer: Poole Studio; Source: National Library of Ireland Ref.: POOLEWP 1329. **THE ROYAL VISIT**; Photographer: Poole Studio; Source: National Library of Ireland Ref.: POOLEWP 1414. **ROCKFIELD PLAYERS**; Photographer: Poole Studio; Source: National Library of Ireland Ref.: POOLEWP 1323. **INFERNAL MACHINE**; Photographer: Poole Studio; Source: National Library of Ireland Ref.: POOLEWP 1494. **WATERFORD BOAT CLUB**; Photographer: Poole Studio; Source: National Library of Ireland Ref.: POOLEWP 1544a. **PEERLESS DE WET**; Photographer: Poole Studio; Source: National Library of Ireland Ref.: POOLEWP 1524. **THE COPPER COAST**; Photographer: Poole Studio; Source: National Library of Ireland Ref.: POOLEWP 1556. **THE POWER OF LOVE**; Photographer: Poole Studio; Source: National Library of Ireland Ref.: POOLEWP 1631a. **BLACKWATER CIDER**; Photographer: Poole Studio; Source: National Library of Ireland Ref.: Poole; N/A. **HOLD A CANDLE**; Photographer: Poole Studio; Source: National Library of Ireland Ref.: POOLEWP 1570. **JONES CHEMIST**; Photographer: Poole Studio; Source: National Library of Ireland Ref.: POOLEWP 1656. **IF THE SUIT FITS**; Photographer: Poole Studio; Source: National Library of Ireland Ref.: POOLEWP 1711. **FORE(!) IN TRAMORE;** Photographer: Poole Studio; Source: National Library of Ireland Ref.: POOLEWP 1694. **LIEUTENANT BECHER**; Photographer: Poole Studio; Source: National Library of Ireland Ref.: POOLEWP 1774a. **THE ROYAL**; Photographer: Poole Studio; Source: National Library of Ireland Ref.: POOLEWP 1824. ***DARTMOUTH CASTLE***; Photographer: Poole Studio; Source: National Library of Ireland Ref.: POOLEWP 1769. **FITZGERALD FAMILY**; Photographer: Poole Studio; Source: National Library of Ireland Ref.: POOLEWP 1961. **COLONIAL HOME**; Photographer: Poole Studio; Source: National Library of Ireland Ref.: POOLEWP 2028. **EVICTION!**; Photographer: Poole Studio; Source: National Library of Ireland Ref.: POOLEWP 2081. **FREEMASONS**; Photographer: Poole Studio; Source: National Library of Ireland Ref.: POOLEWP 2244. **LIFE SAVERS**; Photographer: Poole Studio; Source: National Library of Ireland Ref.: POOLEWP 2062. **DR MARY STRANGMAN**; Photographer: Poole Studio; Source: National Library of Ireland Ref.: POOLEO 7561. **HIGH SHERIFF OF WATERFORD**; Photographer: Poole Studio; Source: National Library of Ireland Ref.: POOLEWP 2264. **REDMOND ELECTED**; Photographer: Poole Studio; Source: National Library of Ireland Ref.: POOLEWP 2123. **TRAMORE HARRIERS**; Photographer: Poole Studio; Source: National Library of Ireland Ref.: Poole; N/A. **ROSAMOND JACOB**; Photographer: Henry Roe McMahon; Source: National Library of Ireland Rosamond Jacob Papers Ref.: MS 33,135/1/5. **DADDY LONG-LEGS**; Photographer: Poole Studio; Source: National Library of Ireland Ref.: POOLEWP 2496. **ADA'S BOUQUET**; Photographer: Poole Studio; Source: National Library of Ireland Ref.: POOLEWP 2527a. **MARCONI ROOM**; Photographer: Poole Studio; Source: National Library of Ireland Ref.: POOLEWP 2539. **FETHARD LIFEBOAT DISASTER**; Photographer: Poole Studio; Source: National Library of Ireland Ref.: POOLEWP 2536. **TORPEDOS AWAY!**; Photographer: Poole Studio; Source: National Library of Ireland Ref.: POOLEWP 0270b. **HORSEMEN & MARSHALS**; Photographer: Poole Studio; Source:

National Library of Ireland Ref.: POOLEWP 2528. **MISS HOOKEY'S TEAM**; Photographer: Poole Studio; Source: National Library of Ireland Ref.: POOLEWP 2627. **CON COLBERT**; Photographer: Keogh Brothers Ltd.; Source: National Library of Ireland Ref.: Ke 212. **SHAMROCKS**; Photographer: Poole Studio; Source: National Library of Ireland Ref.: POOLEWP 2703. **J. MORGAN'S**; Photographer: Poole Studio; Source: National Library of Ireland Ref.: POOLEWP 2658. **THE COUNTESS IN WATERFORD**; Photographer: Poole Studio; Source: National Library of Ireland Ref.: POOLED 4843. **THE WOLFHOUND OF WATERFORD**; Photographer: Poole Studio; Source: National Library of Ireland Ref.: POOLEWP 2708. **HAPPY GLAMPERS**; Photographer: Poole Studio; Source: National Library of Ireland Ref.: POOLEWP 2781. **WILLIAM REDMOND**; Photographer: Poole Studio; Source: National Library of Ireland Redmond Family Ref.: NPA RED8. **MAYOR VINCENT WHITE**; Photographer: Poole Studio; Source: National Library of Ireland Ref.: POOLEWP 2844. **DÉISE DEV**; Photographer: Poole Studio; Source: National Library of Ireland Ref.: POOLEWP 2753. **MICHAEL STAINES**; Photographer: Poole Studio; Source: National Library of Ireland Ref.: POOLED 5740. **PLANE LUCKY**; Photographer: Poole Studio; Source: National Library of Ireland Ref.: POOLEWP 2891. **WACKY RACES**; Photographer: Poole Studio; Source: National Library of Ireland Ref.: POOLEIMP 1696. **DE LA SALLE**; Photographer: Poole Studio; Source: National Library of Ireland Ref.: POOLEWP 2858a. **TOP HATS, TRILBYS AND BOWLERS**; Photographer: Poole Studio; Source: National Library of Ireland Ref.: POOLEWP 2989. **LACEY'S PUBLIC HOUSE**; Photographer: Poole Studio; Source: National Library of Ireland Ref.: POOLEWP 3078. **THE GRANVILLE**; Photographer: Poole Studio; Source: National Library of Ireland Ref.: POOLEWP 3041. **GRACEDIEU**; Photographer: Poole Studio; Source: National Library of Ireland Ref.: POOLEWP 3123. **GLADSTONE STREET CORNER**; Photographer: Poole Studio; Source: National Library of Ireland Ref.: POOLEWP 3175. **FERRYBOAT**; Photographer: Fr Nessan Shaw OFM Cap.; Source: Irish Capuchin Archives Ref.: N/A. **BRENNAN'S**; Photographer: Poole Studio; Source: National Library of Ireland Ref.: POOLEWP 3364. **ST PATRICK'S DAY COMMITTEE**; Photographer: Poole Studio; Source: National Library of Ireland Ref.: POOLEWP 3422. **A CIVIL WELCOME**; Photographer: Poole Studio; Source: National Library of Ireland Ref.: POOLEWP 3548. **PATRICIA**; Photographer: Poole Studio; Source: National Library of Ireland Ref.: POOLEWP 3652a. **MR POOLE**; Photographer: Poole Studio; Source: National Library of Ireland Ref.: POOLEWP 2929a.

*1930–1962*

**SNOW ANGEL**; Photographer: Poole Studio; Source: National Library of Ireland Ref.: POOLEWP 3660. **WOOD NYMPHS**; Photographer: Poole Studio; Source: National Library of Ireland Ref.: POOLEWP 3733. **ADELE ASTAIRE**; Photographer: Unknown; Source: Yesterday's Print Ref.: N/A. **SAINTS AND SINNERS**; Photographer: Poole Studio; Source: National Library of Ireland Ref.: POOLEWP 3910. **BISHOP FOY SCHOOL**; Photographer: Poole Studio; Source: National Library of Ireland Ref.: POOLEWP 3917. **HOW THE SAUSAGE IS MADE!**; Photographer: Poole Studio; Source: National Library of Ireland Ref.: POOLEWP 4245. **H. DOWNES & CO.**; Photographer: Poole Studio; Source: National Library of Ireland Ref.: POOLEWP 4159. **BREAKING NEWS!**; Photographer: Poole Studio; Source: National Library of Ireland Ref.: POOLEWP 4269. **PACKING POWER**; Photographer: Poole Studio; Source: National Library of Ireland; Ref.: Poole; N/A. **WEDDING BELLS**; Photographer: Poole Studio; Source: National Library of Ireland Ref.: POOLEWP 4541. **RYAN'S DAUGHTER**; Photographer: Joe O'Niell; Source: Private Collection Private Ref.: N/A. **FIDDLER AT THE FLEADH**; Photographer: Fáilte Ireland; Source: Irish Traditional Music Archive Ref.: 9706-PH. **LARGE BOTTLE OFF THE SHELF**; Photographer: Tom Tobin; Source: Abbeyside History, Christine Knight O'Connor Tom Tobin, photographer Ref.: N/A. **HEROES OF '59**; Photographer: Annie Brophy; Source: Waterford City Archives / Waterford Treasures / Mount Sion GAA nan Ref.: N/A. **SHOWBAND JOY**; Photographer: Unknown; Source: Corinne Hearne Private Collection Private Ref.: N/A. **TWO COOL DUDES**; Photographer: Joe McGrarh; Source: Jim Lane Private Collection Private Ref.: N/A. **THE POOLE COLLECTION**; Photographer: Poole Studio; Source: National Library of Ireland Ref.: POOLEWP 0173a.